STEAM

Through Five
Continents

The road ahead. The 'Kingston Flyer' waits to leave Fairlight, New Zealand.

October 1991

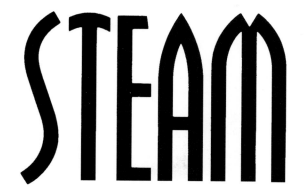

STEAM

Through Five Continents

KEITH STRICKLAND

Foreword by Miles Kington

Acknowledgements

The quotation on page ix is taken from *Far Wheels: A Railroad Safari*, C.S. Small, Cleaver Hume Press, 1959. That on page 90 is taken from the *26th Annual Steam Passenger Service Directory*, Locomotive & Steam Railway Preservation Ltd, 1991. The quotes on pages 119 and 150 are from Paul Theroux's *The Old Patagonian Express*, Hamish Hamilton Ltd, 1979.

A Sutton Publishing Book

This edition published in 1998 by Wrens Park Publishing, an imprint of
W.J. Williams & Son Ltd

First published in the United Kingdom in 1994 by
Alan Sutton Publishing Limited, an imprint of Sutton Publishing Limited
Phoenix Mill · Thrupp · Stroud · Gloucestershire

British Library Cataloguing in Publication Data

A catalogue record for this book is available from the British Library.

ISBN 0905 778 111

Typeset in Baskerville 11/13pt.
Typesetting and origination by
Sutton Publishing Limited.
Printed in Great Britain by
WBC Limited, Bridgend, Mid-Glamorgan.

CONTENTS

British-built steam engines can be found in many parts of the world. Mossman, Queensland, Australia.

September 1993

The weekly 'mixto' from Esquel to Ingeniero Jacobacci fights the grade near El Mayoco, Argentina.

December 1992

FOREWORD

Keith Strickland is a bit like a hunter of a dying species – out there, at the end of the world, there are steam engines still roaming free, and until they are all extinct, he will be drawn to pursue them. There are plenty of steam engines in captivity closer to home, and there are plenty of enthusiasts who will settle for that – indeed, there are plenty of steam enthusiasts who would be far happier repairing a small steam tank engine in a shed up the Severn Valley Railway than haunting a train shed in Paraguay with a camera. But Keith Strickland is made of sterner stuff, and is not happy until he has gone to the far corners of the world to track down the survivors, the trains still working under natural conditions.

What this means, and I don't know if he has realized it, is that Keith Strickland is also a member of a dying species. His fate is tied to that of the steam engine. When the last steam engines have gone from the last main or branch line, obscure private coal mine or tea plantation, there will be nothing for the hunters of steam to pursue, and I don't think they will be happy to settle down in a shed in Bridgnorth and tinker with engines. You can already hear the coming of the end in Keith Strickland's comments on the fading away of steam in India – long thought of as a place where steam could never die – and in his nonchalant forecast that by AD 2000, China will be the only major user of steam anywhere in the world.

Well, it may be the last act of the opera, but it doesn't seem to depress him. In this book he has actually pressed on to new territories like New Zealand, Paraguay and Japan, places where he had never been before, and is still making discoveries of habitats which seem barely credible to me. I had no idea that the Japanese, the most modern people in the world, still had a soft spot for steam. I didn't know that you could still get a steam-driven, *wood-burning* main line in Paraguay. I didn't know that the most southerly refuge of steam was in Argentina, not New Zealand . . .

What Keith Strickland can do for an encore, I cannot think. These roving steam hunters, this dying breed of train-chasers, are as exotic in their own way as the engines they chase. The quite extraordinary thing is that Keith Strickland would have done all this even if he were not putting together a book of photography, and that he and his ilk do it all at their own expense, under their own steam, without ever seeming to think that what they do is extraordinary. Perhaps someone ought to do a book on these strange steam pilgrims before they become extinct and forgotten . . .

Good heavens. Perhaps *that* is what Keith Strickland could do for an encore.

MILES KINGTON
June 1994

Ex-Somerset & Dorset Joint Railway No. 88 runs into Crowcombe station with a train on the West Somerset Railway.

July 1992

INTRODUCTION

'. . . past history . . . is a poor substitute for
the smoke and cinders of reality.'

C.S. Small, *Far wheels: A Railway Safari*

The demise of steam on British Rail in the 1960s affected railway enthusiasts in different ways. Some had no difficulty in transferring their affections to modern traction. Others developed a passion for what steam remained on industrial lines; and many became absorbed by the burgeoning preservation movement. A few, like myself, believed there was no substitute for the real thing and lost interest.

It took me some years to realize that steam could be found in everyday use in many places around the world. Indeed, had I but known, at the time steam finally disappeared on BR in 1968, one had to travel no further than Calais to see steam-hauled express trains.

So it came to pass that one winter's evening in 1974 I boarded a commuter train at Praterstern station in Vienna bound for Ganserndorf, 20 miles north-east of the city. The tank loco at the head was, to my eyes, hardly beautiful; but the familiar smell, sight and sound of steam were all there. The coaches had open balconies and at the end of the front coach, I could stand right next to the engine. As she forged into the cold dark night, sparks shooting from the chimney, the emotional appeal of working steam was rekindled. The atmosphere, the romance and the thrill of steam came flooding back. And there was a new dimension to the excitement – the foreign setting. I was hooked!

Journals and books revealed a long list of countries in which steam was in common use on 'real' railways, as opposed to museum and preserved lines. Later that same year, I spent a long weekend in what was then West Germany enjoying Pacific-hauled expresses and massive 2–10–2s on freights. Next year came Poland. Then India, South Africa, and so on . . . as much as my understanding wife, my bank balance and the exigencies of my job allowed.

Each year, the number of real steam railways decreases. For example, the National Railways of Zimbabwe all but finished with steam in 1993; and it seems that India, long regarded as one of the most interesting steam destinations, will not be far behind. Sometimes changes occur with no apparent warning. Since the chapter on South America was prepared, the situation in Argentina and Paraguay has deteriorated and events referred to in the present tense may be history by the time this book is published.

My travels have included a few countries where there is no steam other than of the preserved variety. Thank goodness Britain is not the only place where the railway's past is appreciated. The preservation of working steam engines will hopefully ensure that future generations will be able to enjoy the sights and sounds which those of us over forty once took for granted.

Photography is an interest which developed out of my travelling. In 1981 I bought second-hand a Pentax Spotmatic F 35 mm SLR camera which by coincidence had originally been sold in 1974, the year of my first foray abroad. All the photographs in this book have been taken with it, using Ilford XP1 or XP2 film.

A first selection of photographs appeared in my last book, *Steam Railways Around the World*. Some of my favourite countries make a second entry here, and the inclusion of several new ones enables all five continents to be featured. Choice of countries is based on one criterion only – personal preference.

The book makes no claim to be representative of steam worldwide, within any one continent, or indeed in a particular country. The photographs have been chosen because I like them!

The warning given in the introduction to my last work needs to be repeated. This book is not a technical treatise. It is intended to convey the general atmosphere of steam railways and the enjoyment to be derived from them. I hope the reader finds as much pleasure in the photographs as I have had in taking and selecting them.

KEITH V. STRICKLAND
April 1994

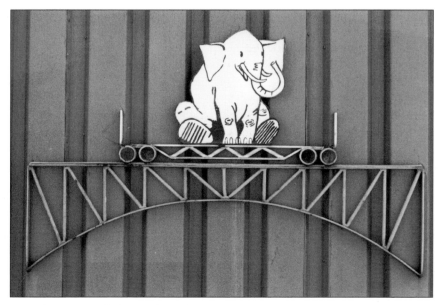

The logo on the gates of the engineering works where steam locomotives were repaired, Bulawayo, Zimbabwe.

July 1989

EUROPE

One of the delights of today's steam scene in Britain is the chance to make good the lost photographic opportunities in the 1950s and 1960s. On a schoolboy's pocket money, I could afford no more than a snapshot camera – an Ilford Sporti. Using 120 roll film, it had two aperture settings – one marked cloudy, the other sunny. To focus, one chose from close-ups, groups and views. Shutter speed was fixed – probably at $1/60$ of a second. With such limited technology, it was no surprise that the end results were disappointing. Any object moving at a speed greater than walking pace was likely to be blurred.

Britain's preserved railways and main line steam specials help to recreate childhood memories. Home was in Somerset, in the heart of Western territory. Holidays brought contact with Southern engines and, in 1962, the lines which now market themselves as the Great Little Trains of Wales.

So began a fondness for narrow gauge steam in general and the Festiniog Railway (FR) in particular. Toy train is a term often applied to narrow gauge railways. While intended to describe the diminutive size of locos and rolling stock compared to standard gauge equipment, the phrase is sometimes used in a derisory fashion in the same way that volunteers are mocked for playing at trains. There is nothing toyish about the Festiniog Railway. It is a professionally run and commercially minded concern. It employs a large number of paid staff and even builds new steam locomotives in its workshops.

In common with the other Welsh narrow gauge lines, the FR runs through magnificent scenery. North Wales is one of the most photogenic areas of the country for steam, except for the rain of which my visits have had their fair share. Despite the weather, the railway attracts thousands of visitors, well over 300,000 in 1993. To the enthusiast, there are special delights. The FR is the longest narrow gauge line in the country, has the only spiral on a passenger line in Britain (discounting miniature railways), and is home to the unique double-ended Fairlie locomotives.

On the standard gauge, the longest preserved line is the West Somerset Railway, a former Great Western branch on which I made countless journeys when a child. It is particularly pleasing that it functions today and that, after a shaky start in the 1970s, it is now thriving.

The first two photographs are of Standard class locomotives introduced by British Railways in the early 1950s. To me, the most pleasing Standard design was the 2–6–4 large tank, of which 155 were built. I only saw six of the class in the flesh, but No. 80054 was the favourite engine on my Hornby Dublo model railway!

No. 70000 *Britannia* leaves Crewe with a special train for Chester.

July 1991

Standard 2–6–4 tank No. 80079 approaches Bridgnorth on the Severn Valley Railway.

March 1983

At Crewe Heritage Centre, No. 777 *Sir Lamiel* is prepared prior to working a train to Holyhead. No. 777 is a 4–6–0 of the 'King Arthur' class introduced by the Southern Railway in 1925. To the left is *Flying Scotsman*. The cars were participants in a vintage transport event.

July 1991

Special events are a regular feature of the steam calendar. The Great Western Society's museum at Didcot holds an annual night-photography session. Locos are positioned to benefit from specially installed lighting. The floodlight on the water tower produces an interesting effect. There's a nip in the air and the brazier has been fired to prevent the water crane from freezing.

October 1987

No. 5051 *Earl Bathurst* (otherwise known as *Drysllwyn Castle*) climbs the last mile to Sapperton Tunnel with a Gloucester to Swindon train. Rain was sweeping across the Cotswolds and my camera nearly stayed in its bag. But the sight of a 'Castle' hard at work was too good to miss. By uprating my film to 1000 ASA, I was able to use a fast enough shutter speed to freeze movement and to capture the atmosphere of a wet summer's day.

August 1985

A few weeks later, the weather was kinder. Moments before Nos 5051 and 7029 *Clun Castle* came into view, the sun burst through an overcast sky to bathe the countryside in soft evening light. The two 'Castles' are approaching Cogload signal box east of Taunton with a train for Bristol. This was a much frequented spot in the 1950s. The routes to the West Country from Bristol and from Westbury converged at Cogload, and just to the rear of the train there used to be water troughs. It was always a thrill to watch locos pick up water at speed. Happy memories!

September 1985

Small 2–6–2 tanks could be found at work on ex-Great Western branch lines throughout the West Country. No. 4566 is preserved on the Severn Valley Railway where she is seen emerging from the tunnel between Kidderminster and Bewdley . . .

April 1987

. . . and approaching Victoria Bridge. The train is an all-stations stopper so someone has made a mistake in using the headlamp code for an express.

April 1987

Locos running tender first don't make very good pictures and are often ignored by photographers. Broadside views are an exception, the more so if set against an attractive background. No. 88 in Somerset & Dorset black livery nears Combe Florey on the West Somerset Railway.

July 1992

Three years earlier, No. 88 was in BR colours. There is an appreciative group of onlookers as she runs round her train at Bishops Lydeard.

August 1989

In recent years, the West Somerset Railway has played host to visiting engines. *City of Truro* was a popular choice in 1992. She achieved fame as the first locomotive in the world to reach 100 m.p.h. – or so it is claimed. In high summer, she nears the top of the climb from Bishops Lydeard to Crowcombe.

July 1992

A famous nameplate.

July 1992

There is no mistaking the family connection between *City of Truro* at Bishops Lydeard . . .

July 1992

. . . and *Earl of Berkeley* at Didcot Museum.

October 1987

One of the two 2–4–0 tanks built in 1902 for the opening of the Welshpool & Llanfair Light Railway, and still at work on the line. She waits to leave Llanfair Caereinion with the first train of the day for Welshpool.

April 1987

In contrast, this 2–6–2 tank is a long way from her original territory. Built by Hunslet in 1954, she worked in Sierra Leone until that country abandoned its railway in 1974. She crosses the River Banwy with a train which includes coaches from Austria and Sierra Leone.

April 1987

The Festiniog Railway's extensive workshops are at Boston Lodge. *Blanche* looks upset at being wheel-less. Built by Hunslet of Leeds in 1893, she worked on the Penrhyn Railway taking slate from quarries to the coast until closure of that line in 1962.

September 1983

One of the double-ended Fairlies. *Merddin Emrys*, on a Down train at Tan-y-Bwlch, was originally constructed at Boston Lodge in 1879.

September 1983

Spot the train! Participants on a railway photographers' weekend held at the Snowdonia National Park Study Centre prepare for action on a typically wet and windy day.

September 1983

Just as the rain stops for the first time in two days, an Up train climbs Gwyndy bank hauled by *Earl of Merioneth*, built at Boston Lodge in 1979 – yes, 1979.

September 1983

AFRICA

At the age of ten or thereabouts, I was given the *Eagle Book of Trains*. In it were some colour sectionalized drawings showing the innards of steam locomotives. One was a 'Garratt' of South African Railways (SAR). This bore little resemblance to any engine I had ever seen. It seemed improbable that such a massive machine could run on a gauge no wider than 3 ft 6 in, but that is what the caption claimed.

Africa was an exotic faraway place to someone who had never been outside the West Country. I didn't imagine for a minute that one day I would visit the continent; but that drawing made a vivid impression and was never forgotten.

In the 1970s the Republic of South Africa was much visited and photographed by British enthusiasts. As someone put it, it was a country where white men and black engines ruled supreme. Most gricers gave little thought to the iniquities and injustices perpetuated by the former. One avoided political considerations, and concentrated on the latter. As late as 1979 it was possible to see over six hundred steam locos on a two week holiday. Now, when it is no longer politically incorrect to visit the country, regular steam has gone, except on some industrial lines. Fortunately, the preservation movement flourishes. Main line steam specials run regularly giving one the chance to photograph working steam in beautiful surroundings.

South Africa provided my first 'Garratt' in the flesh. But, as everyday steam on SAR declined in the 1980s, Zimbabwe became the mecca for 'Garratt' enthusiasts. The National Railways of Zimbabwe kept steam going throughout the decade. On and off, it was the main source of motive power on three of the routes out of Bulawayo.

After legal independence and the end of guerilla fighting, travel within Zimbabwe presented few problems. To the determined lineside photographer, the best way of getting around was to hire a car. The technique was to follow the railway as closely as possible (often on dirt roads), find a train, and then chase it. Train speeds were low and most lines were single track, necessitating lengthy crossing stops. It was fairly easy to leapfrog a train to capture more than one shot of it.

Two weeks in Zimbabwe in 1989 provided almost a surfeit of 'Garratts' amidst the splendour of the African bush. At times one almost wished for the monotony to be broken by a conventional loco!

The icing on the cake (not a very appropriate metaphor given the climate) was the opportunity to ride in the cab on both passenger and freight trains. The rides were no short hops but complete journeys – five hours long in one case – a far cry from the days of dreaming over the *Eagle Book of Trains*.

Victoria Falls station. No. 377 is a 4–6–4 + 4–6–4. I have just climbed down from her cab
after riding from Thomson Junction with an afternoon freight.

July 1989

Conveniently situated on a hill overlooking the main line from Thomson Junction to Bulawayo, the Baobab Hotel at Hwange was much patronized by steam enthusiasts. From below . . .

July 1989

. . . and from above. There is a marvellous panorama from the gardens of the hotel.

July 1989

Trains crossing at Figtree. From ground level . . .

July 1989

. . . and from the cab of the loco on the daily all-stations passenger train from Plumtree to Bulawayo.

July 1989

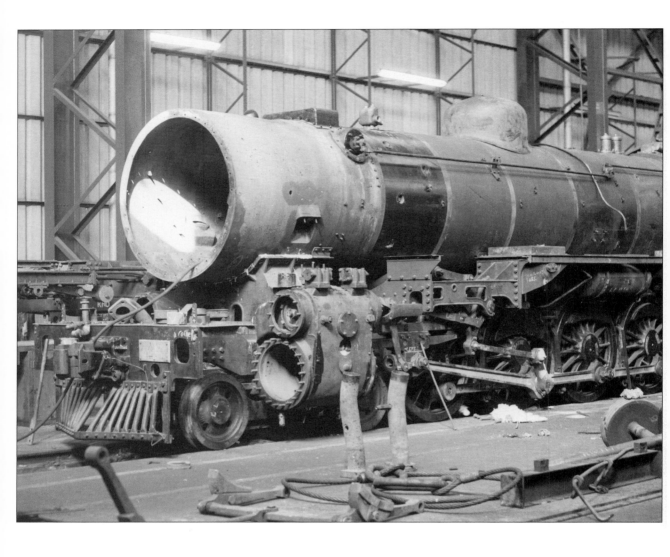

Major overhauls were undertaken at Zeco, a steel construction firm in Bulawayo.

July 1989

No. 4 is a 4–8–2 owned by Wankie Colliery.

July 1989

First light at Bulawayo engine sheds. A magical atmosphere. No. 741 is a 4–8–2 + 2–8–4.

July 1989

No. 510 has a 2–6–2 + 2–6–2 wheel arrangement. Bulawayo sheds.

July 1989

Thomson Junction.

July 1989

Bulawayo.

July 1989

No. 424 makes a fine sight as she nears Syringa with a freight from Plumtree to Bulawayo.

July 1989

No. 415 near Entuba with coal for Bulawayo.

July 1989

The massive proportions of a 'Garratt' are evident in this photograph. Remember – this is on a gauge of 3 ft 6 in. Figtree.

July 1989

No. 613, a 2–8–2 + 2–8–2, pauses at Mbalabala on the West Nicholson branch. The rock outcrops are a distinctive feature of the area.

July 1989

The last rays of the setting sun catch No. 424 as she storms through Sandown on the
Plumtree–Bulawayo line.

July 1989

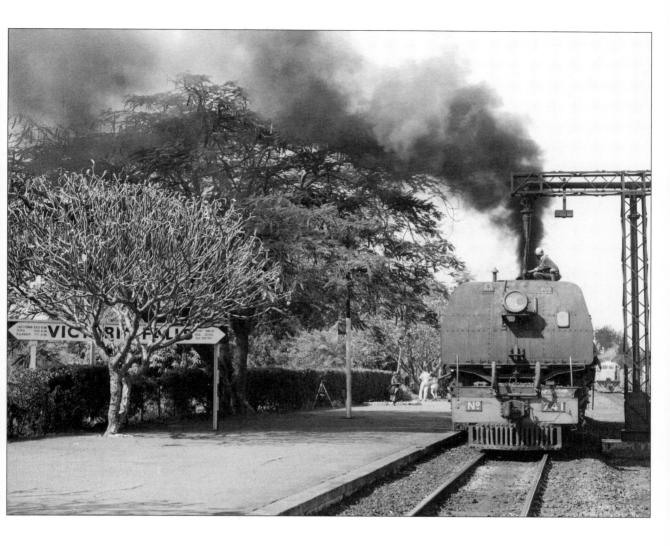

No. 741 has just arrived at Victoria Falls, with a freight from Thomson Junction. The sign reads:

Cape Town	2651 km
Beira	1534 km
Bulawayo	451 km

and gives the height of the station as 913 m above sea level. This line was part of Cecil Rhodes' dream of a Cape to Cairo route, never to be fulfilled. The railway crosses into Zambia on a bridge over the Zambezi River built close enough to the Victoria Falls for spray to hit the carriages – at Rhodes' specific instruction, so legend says.

July 1989

Across the border in Zambia lies the town of Livingstone. It's strange how the town's name has survived the colonial era. Livingstone was the first non-African to see the Falls. Photographically, 'dead' steam locos offer little appeal to me, but I liked this composition at the town's railway museum.

July 1989

ASIA

Of all the countries to which my travels have taken me – well over thirty now – those of the Indian Sub-Continent hold the greatest fascination. It's not easy to say precisely why. Certainly, the railways are a factor. So is the British connection. Nearly half a century after independence, there is still much evidence of the Raj, not least in railway practice and equipment. Ultimately though, it's the fascination of cultures and of a way of life so different from ours in the West.

Whole books and TV documentaries have been written about the railways of India. There is even a society devoted entirely to the subject. Throughout the 1970s and 1980s, India was one of the prime destinations for steam buffs. Unfortunately, steam is now on the way out and by the end of the century the country may well see no more than a few tourist operations. On the plus side, there will be no shortage of photographs and films to recall the romance of Indian steam. (Incidentally, one of the most vivid descriptions in writing of a footplate journey is found in John Masters' novel *Bhowani Junction*, set in pre-independence India.)

Sri Lanka is an unlikely place to find preserved steam. On the broad gauge (5 ft 6 in, the same as in India), steam finished in the 1970s. Fortunately some locos escaped being cut up, and turntables and water columns were left *in situ*. Due to the enthusiasm and commitment of an English travel agent, a local counterpart and the general manager of the railway, a few engines were restored, and in 1986 the first steam-hauled tourist train ran, called the 'Viceroy Special'.

There are four broad gauge steam locos in working order, all built in England. Railway buildings and signalling equipment reflect British design; and riding the 'Viceroy Special', one can easily imagine what train travel was like in pre-war colonial Ceylon.

Come the year 2000, China will be the one remaining major user of steam locos. Indeed, the construction of new steam engines continued throughout the 1980s. To the enthusiast, standardization has reduced much of the appeal. A few classes account for most of the locos, though more variety can be found on industrial lines.

For somewhere long considered to be in the forefront of technological development, Japan continued to use steam on her railways surprisingly late – well into the 1970s in fact. Since then the national railways have had the good sense to retain some steam locos and to run them as tourist attractions.

The Japanese are very railway minded. They take great pride not only in their modern high-speed trains but also in their railway heritage. They are delighted when others, too, show an interest, and any Western rail buff who makes it to Japan is assured of a welcome.

There can be no mistaking the class 'WP' Pacifics on India's broad gauge (5 ft 6 in). The bullet nose, invariably decorated with the Star of India, is more for effect than for a practical purpose. Indian trains don't run at high speeds and have no need of streamlining. Agra.

November 1985

Class 'WG' No. 9821 is a 2–8–2 freight loco built in India as recently as 1961, though one wouldn't guess so from its unkempt appearance. Lucknow.

November 1985

On the metre gauge, classes 'YP' and 'YG' are the standard Pacifics and 2–8–2s. 'YP'
No. 2586 takes water at Bandikui on train '22 Down', the 5.45 a.m. express from Jaipur to
Agra.

November 1985

'YG' No. 3418 at Bandikui.

November 1985

Varanasi metre gauge shed.

November 1985

Double-headed trains are not a common sight in India. 'YP' No. 2447 and an unidentified class 'YL' 2–6–2 enter Jaipur. The time of day and the auxiliary water tanks suggest this is the daily train from Toda Rai Singh.

November 1985

Up-country among the tea plantations for which Sri Lanka is famous, the 'Viceroy Special' leaves Nanu Oya bound for Kandy.

February 1994

No. 340 *Frederick North* is a 4–6–0 built in 1945.

February 1994

Apart from the metal-bodied first coach and the concrete sleepers, this could be a scene from the 1930s. No. 213 is a 4–6–0 tender tank locomotive constructed by Vulcan Foundry in 1922. Near Rambukkana.

February 1994

The line from Kandy to Badulla runs through Sri Lanka's spectacular hill country on gradients as steep as 1 in 45. No. 340 pulls out of one of the wayside stations between Kandy and Hatton. This route provided some exhilarating night-time footplate rides on No. 340.

February 1994

Peradeniya Junction.

February 1994

There is one 2 ft 6 in gauge railway in Sri Lanka, the Kelani Valley line from Colombo, though it is currently being converted to broad gauge. Pride of the line is this Sentinel steam railcar, the only one of its type at work today anywhere in the world. Built at Shrewsbury in 1928, it was restored in 1990 and is now used for special charters. Kottawa.

February 1994

A narrow gauge train from Colombo to Avissawella near the Royal Colombo Golf Club, behind 4–6–4 No. 220 built by Hunslet in 1924. The line runs slap through the middle of the course, to the mutual annoyance of railway photographers and golfers.

February 1994

Homagama.

February 1994

Mention Sri Lanka, and most people think of Buddhist monks . . . . Kadugannawa.

February 1994

. . . and elephants. Rambukkana.

February 1994

An unusual view of the two locos at the head of the 'Viceroy Special' as it arrives at Hatton.
Throughout the sub-continent, children are fascinated by the antics of steam enthusiasts.

February 1994

Tunnel-like conditions on the double-decker bridge across the Yangtze River at Wuhan, China. With the camera at rail level, it was possible to turn depth-of-field difficulties to advantage to create an impression of power and speed.

December 1982

Class 'QJ' 2–10–2 No. 6112 on a freight near Guilin.

December 1982

In 1982, Datong loco workshops were building 'QJ's at the rate of one a day. A brand new 'QJ', No. 6396, fresh from the paint shop, sits in the steam testing plant.

Here was another photographic challenge – black engine, dark surroundings, no tripod! The solution was to concentrate on the parts of the subject lit by the limited amount of natural light, select a slow shutter speed, pray for a steady hand, and trust to luck.

December 1982

Problems of a different kind – a profusion of wires and poles. Pacific class 'RM' No. 1182 pulls out of Taiyuan with a passenger train.

December 1982

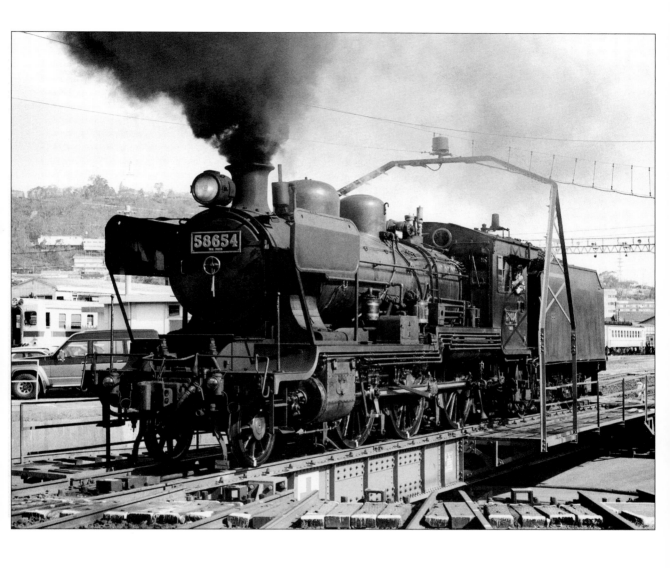

The only regular steam operation on Kyushu, the southernmost of Japan's main islands, is based at Kumamoto. In the tourist season, trains run most days to Miyaji. This is no half-hearted affair. The single track line has a frequent diesel passenger service, and the steam train must keep to time. In addition, there are some steep gradients including a zig-zag. Kumamoto shed.

October 1992

Kumamoto.

October 1992

At the foot of the zig-zag.

October 1992

AUSTRALASIA

New Zealand Railways (NZR) has not used steam for many years but for a country of only three million or so people, there is a surprising amount of interest in the preservation movement. Steam specials on the main line are commonplace, and there are many museum sites and lines in both North and South Islands.

From Britain, New Zealand is the farthest one can go for steam. The rewards are well worth the time and effort. Apart from the locomotives themselves, the country offers a staggering variety of scenery – from sub-tropical beaches in the north to mountains and glaciers in the south.

Then there is the friendliness of the people. Some visitors say, in a derogatory way, that New Zealand is thirty years behind the times. If by this they mean life is lived at a leisurely pace and that there is an old-fashioned courtesy, this is to everyone's credit. You will certainly be given a big welcome. New Zealanders appreciate the fact that you've travelled half-way round the globe to get there. One word of advice to teetotallers and vegetarians: the country produces some excellent wines, and there is rather a lot of lamb on the menu.

NZR tracks are 3 ft 6 in. As in South Africa, a generous loading gauge enabled locomotive designers to produce machines of massive proportions. They had to be big to generate sufficient power to cope with the switchback gradients.

Early locos were purchased from British and American manufacturers, but NZR developed their own construction business. Local enthusiasts are intensely proud of the home-built engines which have survived into the preservation era.

Some locos have had remarkable lives. Years ago, NZR were in the habit of dumping scrapped engines and wagons into river beds to prevent erosion of banks. In recent years, at least one American loco over a century old has been recovered from a wet grave and restored to running condition. No mean achievement.

There is one item of transport in the South Island which, though non-railway, should not be missed by a steam enthusiast: the TSS Earnslaw (Twin Screw Steamer). Built in 1912, powered by two locomotive-type coal-fired boilers, and retaining her original wood panelling and brass fittings, she cruises Lake Wakatipu. You will not be disappointed, especially if invited to visit the engine room.

Australia is represented by the Port Douglas & Mossman Steam Railway. This is one of the many 2 ft gauge sugar lines in Queensland. The railway was originally built to transport sugar cane from fields to the processing mill, and the finished product from the mill to the coast. The mill at Mossman still brings in cane by rail, though with diesel power. Steam-hauled tourist trains run in the season in connection with guided visits to the mill.

Mossman.

September 1993

This 0–6–0 isn't as old as she looks, having been built by the Leeds firm of Hudswell Clarke in 1950. Mossman Mill.

September 1993

Of the locos currently on the Port Douglas & Mossman Railway, *Bundy* is the only one which worked at the mill in steam days. She is an 0–6–2 built at the Bundaberg Foundry in Queensland in 1952. The tender is a later addition. Port Douglas.

September 1993

Bundy on a train from Mossman to Port Douglas.

September 1993

On shed, Port Douglas.

September 1993

New Zealand's class 'Ka' 4–8–4s stand nearly 12 ft tall. For a time, they carried a semi-streamlined casing. This gave them a vastly different appearance at the front end from the unadulterated version. No. 942 takes water at Te Kuiti on the main trunk line through North Island.

October 1991

'Ka' 945 at Paekakariki shed.

October 1991

Though No. 942 burns oil, her fire is lit with kindling. Auckland.

October 1991

The fireman's son gives a helping hand. Auckland.

October 1991

This elegant machine, a class 'Ab' Pacific built in NZR's own workshops in 1925, hauls the 'Kingston Flyer', a tourist train on South Island. The driver puts on quite a show at the Kingston terminus. So well balanced is the turntable, he only needs to give an initial push.

October 1991

Kingston.

October 1991

Nine of us chartered the 'Flyer' and had it to ourselves for a whole morning. I rode in the cab and the driver obligingly provided run-pasts wherever asked. Blue sky, crystal-clear air, wonderful scenery, snow on the mountain tops, white steam and a gleaming loco combined to provide a memorable experience.

October 1991

Climbing out of Kingston.

October 1991

Waiting to leave Fairlight.

October 1991

Backlighting has enhanced the smoke effects. Kingston.

October 1991

No. 16 is a 2–4–0 wood-burner built in Glasgow by Neilson & Sons Ltd way back in 1878.
Today she runs on the Pleasant Point Railway in South Island.

October 1991

No. 16's fireperson.

October 1991

On the outskirts of Christchurch, the Ferrymead Trust operates both a tramway and a railway. No. 7 is an 0–4–0 steam tram loco. Constructed in 1881 by Kitsons of Leeds, it is thought to be the only one of its kind still working in the world. The wheels are concealed by 'skirts'.

October 1991

A product of the Scottish firm of Sharp Stewart, this 0–6–0 will celebrate her centenary in 1997. Shantytown.

October 1991

The Glenbrook Vintage Railway (GVR) lies in North Island. No. 1250 is an NZR 4–8–2; No. 4 is a 2–4–4–2 'Mallet' of obvious American extraction built for the lumber industry. Pukeoware.

October 1991

The turnout of loco and guard reflects the pride of the GVR's staff, all volunteers. Fernleigh.

October 1991

No. 4 on a train for Glenbrook.

October 1991

No. 4 was built by the American Locomotive Company in 1913.

October 1991

NORTH AMERICA

Railway preservation in the USA is thriving according to the *Annual Steam Passenger Service Directory*. This American publication lists well over two hundred locations though close inspection reveals that these include trams (or trolleys in local parlance). America has a great interest and pride in its past, and Americans are capable of levels of sentimentality to match those of the British. Take this quotation from the 1991 directory:

> Steam locomotives inspire passion, no doubt because of their humanlike qualities. They show the effort of their labor by puffing and panting, appearing to breathe faster and faster as they gain speed, telling us by their thundering exhaust when they are straining under a heavy load.

US steam is represented here by three lines in the states of Colorado and New Mexico, chosen because of the magnificent mountain scenery through which they run. The most notable feature of the Georgetown Loop Railroad is the curved Devil's Gate Viaduct, part of a 360° spiral by which the line gains height in a narrow valley. The railroad has two 'Shays', geared locos designed to haul heavy loads at slow speed over severe gradients, and much used by logging companies.

The Durango & Silverton Narrow Gauge and Cumbres & Toltec Scenic Railroads were once part of the Denver & Rio Grande's (D & RG) extensive 3 ft gauge system. Both lines operate original D & RG 2–8–2s (Mikado is the name for this wheel arrangement) of typical American appearance – rugged beauty is the most charitable description.

In contrast is the former Canadian Pacific engine now known as the *Royal Hudson*. With stainless steel cladding to the boiler, fire-box and cylinders, and a livery of maroon and black, she is an elegant machine. Hudson is the term for a 4–6–4 wheel arrangement. One of the class hauled the royal train on a visit by King George VI to Canada – hence the name *Royal Hudson*. The locomotive was built in Montreal in 1940. Now owned by the Government of British Columbia, in the summer she runs from North Vancouver to Squamish.

Much of the *Royal Hudson*'s route is alongside the Howe Sound, a fjord-like inlet of the sea. With mountains on one side and water on the other, it is a magnificent trip, made particularly memorable by the railway authority's kindness in allowing my wife and myself to ride the footplate.

No. 14 is one of the two 'Shays' on the Georgetown Loop RR. Silver Plume.

June 1990

The other 'Shay', on the Devil's Gate Viaduct, going Up . . .

June 1990

. . . and coming Down.

June 1990

On the Durango & Silverton RR, No. 481 is outward bound from Durango.

June 1990

She is seen again at Rockwood on the return journey.

June 1990

A meet on the outskirts of Silverton.

June 1990

Silverton.

June 1990

The old depot (i.e. station) at Silverton.

June 1990

Silverton recedes into the distance as No. 481 begins the traverse of the Animas River gorge, 25 miles in length.

June 1990

Rugged beauty. Rockwood.

June 1990

Approaching Rockwood with an early morning train for Silverton.

June 1990

Of photographs taken by leaning out of a moving train, no more than one in a hundred is a success. The Animas River gorge.

June 1990

Returning home to Durango in soft evening light.

June 1990

Chama, the western terminus of the Cumbres & Toltec Scenic RR.

June 1990

Extra coaches have been attached to the daily train from Chama to Antonito, necessitating a
pilot loco.

June 1990

Lobato. The Rio Grande name has been applied to the tender of the leading engine – a nice touch.

June 1990

Looking down into Wolf Creek from Windy Point. Climbing steeply, the train is about to enter a huge horseshoe curve. After two miles, it will appear behind *and above* the photographer's viewpoint!

June 1990

Approaching the summit at Cumbres.

June 1990

At Cumbres, the pilot engine has been detached and is about to return to Chama light engine. According to the marker board, the station is 10,015 ft above sea-level.

June 1990

One of the distinctive American-style water tanks on the Cumbres & Toltec RR. Osier.

June 1990

Equally typical of US railroad design is the caboose (i.e. guard's van). Chama.

June 1990

No. 2860 *Royal Hudson*. Squamish.

August 1993

Britannia Beach.

August 1993

No. 2860's engineer (left) and stoker – driver and fireman in British terminology. Squamish.

August 1993

Oiling round at Squamish.

August 1993

En route to Squamish.

August 1993

A view from the cab approaching one of the numerous curves on the shores of Howe Sound.

August 1993

The Canadian Pacific operated not only a trans-continental railway but shipping on the Atlantic and Pacific Oceans. The badge claims that the company 'spans the world'. From the dizzy heights of No. 2860's cab, my wife felt queen of all she surveyed!

August 1993

SOUTH AMERICA

Steam Railways Around the World included photographs taken in Brazil, Chile and Peru. In the book, I remarked wistfully that I had only been to South America once. That state of affairs has now been remedied and three more countries added to the collection.

Paraguay's standard gauge railway has the grand title Ferrocarril Presidente Carlos Antonio Lopez. (South Americans have a habit of naming places and things after public figures.) From the capital Asuncion, it runs some 230 miles to Encarnacion where it crosses the River Parana into Argentina.

How does the railway manage to survive? Track, equipment, buildings – all have an air of decrepitude. Trains are infrequent, run hours late and are often derailed. This is hardly surprising since most of the track is laid directly onto the earth. And pervading all aspects of the line's operation is the *mañana* factor.

Perversely, this laid-back approach is part of the railway's attraction, if a little frustrating at times. The apparent dereliction adds fascination to a set-up which is 100 per cent steam and, moreover, uses wood as the prime type of fuel. Steam-hauled international passenger trains are rare in themselves. One pulled by a wood-burner is probably unique.

At the time of writing, Argentina has two lines worked entirely by steam. Both are in deepest Patagonia. It takes a great deal of time and effort to reach them but the rewards are great, for they provide two of the most satisfying steam experiences currently on offer worldwide. Catch them before it is too late!

At 52 °S and just above the Straits of Magellan, the 75 cm (approx. 2 ft 6 in) Ramal Ferro Industrial Rio Turbio (RFIRT) is the most southerly railway in the world. There is no regular passenger traffic. The railway transports coal from mines at Rio Turbio 160 miles eastwards through bleak and uninhabited country to the coast at Rio Gallegos, from where it is taken by sea to Buenos Aires. A fleet of 2–10–2s built in Japan by Mitsubishi in 1956 and 1963 haul remarkable loads for such a narrow gauge.

The *pièce de résistance* (or its Spanish equivalent) is the Esquel branch of what was once the Ferrocarril General Roca. Starting at Ingeniero Jacobacci, a junction on the broad gauge line to Bariloche, the 75 cm gauge track twists, turns, climbs and dives for 250 miles before reaching Esquel. This is a bleak area – semi-desert, very thinly populated, and poor. Paul Theroux finished his marathon train journey through the Americas here. He thought the landscape had a prehistoric look, like 'a painted backdrop for a dinosaur skeleton in a museum'. This is the place to go to see steam trains in a dramatic setting.

Encarnacion station, Paraguay.

December 1992

Most of Paraguay's locos burn wood. Asuncion shed.

December 1992

The colonial-style architecture of the terminus at Asuncion contrasts sharply with the surrounding high-rise properties. A road cuts the main platform in two. 2–6–0 No. 102 eases a short train across the level-crossing.

December 1992

After leaving Asuncion's station, the railway runs down the middle of one of the city's side streets. No. 102 was built by the North British Locomotive Co. in 1910.

December 1992

The railway's workshops are at Sapucai.

December 1992

San Salvador is the junction for the Abai branch, and has a small shed.

December 1992

San Salvador.

December 1992

San Salvador.

December 1992

Between Villarica and San Salvador.

December 1992

No. 59 pauses at José Fassardi with a special train on the Abai branch. The last coach is an old wooden-bodied diner. It has been splendidly restored and refurbished, but lunch in a room temperature of 102 °F was a little uncomfortable. Among the kit carried on the engine's running plate and bufferbeam are tool boxes, jacks, a bucket of sand and a length of hosepipe.

December 1992

Somewhere on the Abai branch. In theory the pump in the river uses steam from the loco to force water up into the tender. On this occasion it didn't work. End of journey!

December 1992

Nos 4 and 120 account for two-thirds of Uruguay's fleet of working steam locos. No. 4, built by Beyer Peacock, is 105 years old. Seen here with auxiliary tender, she is a 2–6–0 tank. Florida.

December 1992

In many parts of South America, the earliest railways were financed, constructed and operated by British companies. There can be no mistaking this engine's British parentage. She is another product of Beyer Peacock. Although carrying No. 120, she is actually No. 119. Florida.

December 1992

Cardal.

December 1992

There are no regular passenger trains out of Uruguay's capital, Montevideo. Steam specials therefore generate quite a stir. Cardal.

December 1992

The RFIRT shed at Rio Gallegos. My locally produced map of the area (entitled 'The map of the end of the world') is not detailed enough to tell whether this or the shed at the other end of the line is the southernmost loco depot on the globe. Someone will no doubt tell me.

December 1992

Rio Gallegos, Argentina.

December 1992

No. 107 is from the first batch of 2–10–2s purchased in 1956. Rio Gallegos.

December 1992

Rio Gallegos.

December 1992

Rio Turbio shed.

December 1992

No. 104 forges out of Rio Gallegos with a rake of empties for Rio Turbio.

December 1992

The same train between Rio Gallegos and Bella Vista.

December 1992

There's just one passenger train a week on Argentina's Esquel branch. At the end of 1992 it ran from Ingeniero Jacobacci to Esquel on Fridays and returned on Saturdays. Journey time was supposed to be about 14 hours, but breakdowns and delays were frequent.

The Saturday train pauses at Nahuel Pan, a station typically in the middle of nowhere.

December 1992

Later, near Lepa . . .

December 1992

. . . and not far from El Maiten. The third vehicle is a restaurant car. Lunch the previous day was cold meats and the hearts of palm fronds, spaghetti, steak, and strawberries and cream, accompanied by good red wine. Where else in the world could one dine so well behind double-headed steam on the 2 ft 6 in gauge?

December 1992

Apart from the El Maiten works shunter, all the line's locos are 2–8–2s, some built by Baldwin (USA) the remainder by Henschel (Germany). A Baldwin leads a Henschel on a chartered mixed train at El Maiten in Chubut Province.

December 1992

Luck plays a part in photography. Had the smoke been thicker it would have blotted out the mountains. Between El Maiten and Norquinco.

December 1992

Not far from Norquinco.

December 1992

Last light, El Maiten shed.

December 1992

The end of the week's work, El Maiten.

December 1992

'. . . beside the desert the labouring engine chugged, always seeming on the verge of spewing its guts out, exploding in a shower of metal and vapour, or else seizing up in a succession of glugs. . . . It seemed a marvel that an old engine like this could keep going. . . .' – Paul Theroux
The Esquel branch, Argentina.

December 1992